THE
GORILLA
AND THE
FAIRY

Written and Illustrated

by

Carol Young

HARA
PUBLISHING
Seattle, Washington

Published by
Hara Publishing
P.O. Box 19732
Seattle, WA 98109
(425) 775-7868

ISBN: 1-883697-53-0
LC: 2002100346

Manufactured in Korea
10 9 8 7 6 5 4 3 2

Illustrations and Book Design by
Carol Young

DEDICATION

This book is dedicated to my angels. Family and friends who believed in me even when I couldn't. Thank you for holding me and listening to me for hours and most of all making me aware of how valuable I really am. Sometimes we all need to be reminded. I will never forget you.

CAROL

THE GORILLA AND THE FAIRY

She lived in the meadow next to the dark forest. A beautiful little Fairy with pearlescent wings and tiny delicate white feet. She enjoyed painting the flowers with nutrients and tending to them as fairies do. Fairies, like all other beings of the light, are healers and nurturers.

The meadow was a magical place. Awakening each morning wrapped warmly in a rose petal, the Fairy would stretch her wings with a flutter, wash her face in a dew drop and slide down the end of a rainbow into a flock of fairies twirling on the breeze, having the ride of their lives. She would kiss every blossom awake and sing sweetly to all the creatures of the meadow as the sun warmed the early morning air. Life was full of joy in the meadow.

He was the most powerful animal living in the dark forest adjacent to the meadow. He could hardly contain his own strength. He hated the meadow, hated the light.

He had ruled his dark domain through intimidation. If he was seen in the light the other creatures of the forest would see he was not as strong as they thought. He could never let that happen. He loved the control their fear gave him.

Early one evening he sat with his head in his hands. He was lonely and empty, a dull pain ached inside him. Life did not feel so good. Something was missing. As he glanced up he saw splashes of light flickering in a swarm, like fireflies. He stared for the longest time in awe of the scene playing out in front of him. Then he saw her.

She had wandered into the dark forest, drawn by violets that needed tending. He had never seen a fairy before. He had heard stories about fairies and elves and other creatures when he was young, but he never really believed they existed. He watched with wonder as she gently tended to the violets. At that moment, he decided he must possess her. He did not worry, for he always got what he wanted, yet he knew he must be careful because fairies could sense his darkness.

$\mathcal{S}$o he dug into his very soul to find the last remnants of good he possessed — to trick her into being his.

She felt his presence. At first it startled her! She froze. He was so intense, so intimidating. She felt a chill run through her, and for a moment she felt a desperate need to fly away. Then she noticed a small speck of blue light glowing from his heart, and she could feel his pain. In compassion she slowly floated toward him, focusing on the light to keep her from being afraid.

She spoke in a soft, sweet voice. "Don't be afraid." Her gentle non-threatening way overwhelmed him and the light she radiated gave warmth, safety and excitement. He loved the way she made him feel. Almost instantly his small blue light flared in intensity. Although he was not capable of giving, and his light burned blue and cloudy, still it was a light. He had not been taught to care for or respect life, only to *take and control*. He would do anything to win her, *anything to win!*

The Fairy had been raised to be trusting. Her natural inclination was to help this creature find his soul. That evening she had him climb to the top of the highest tree in the forest. Here he took in the breathtaking intensity of the colors of the sunset.

3

$\mathcal{S}$he showed him the dance of the fireflies and the rebirth of a flower. It was as if he had been blind and was just given sight. He had never looked for beauty before. Time passed quickly as each joyful moment led to another. She encouraged him, telling him he was brave and unique. She was the only one who had ever believed in him, or for that matter, treated him with such respect and kindness.

His eyes softened and sparkled. One single tear slid down his cheek and he looked at her as if she was the most beautiful creature he had ever seen. He told her he was falling in love with her and begged her to stay. She was so moved by his new awareness of love that she promised she would.

For the first time, he felt like a child. He brought her rocks in the shape of hearts, all polished and smooth. He ran with her to the edge of an old bog deep in the forest, to show her the reflection of a full moon peeking through the dense foliage. He told her he had captured the moon as a gift for her, confessing that even heaven thought they belonged together. He held her very gently as if she were made of crystal and promised to always protect her. So taken was he by the little Fairy that he thought he could hide his dark side from her forever. Over time she fell in love with the Gorilla. She didn't listen when the wind warned her, *"Don't trust him!"* She didn't listen when the forest sang to her, *"Run away!"*

He seemed to try so hard that she stopped looking at him with her eyes and felt only the small glimpse of his soul that he chose to share with her. Her heart looked at him though filters of love and, blinded by her own loving spirit, she saw him as beautiful. She saw his strength and warmth. She believed in him. The forest was wrong.

In time, he drew her closer and closer. Without the light and love from her family and friends, and in the darkness of the forest, she began to need to have his arms surround her to protect her. He told her the wind was not her friend and that only he loved her. She was glad she was warm and safe in his arms in this dark, cold place.

She didn't realize that he never really intended for the light to grow within him. He wouldn't be able to rule the forest if the other creatures knew his need for the little Fairy. He played his little game and before she knew it, she was his possession, his most valuable possession. He certainly did not want to live without her. For the first time, he felt loved, cared for and valued. At the same time, he needed to control her— so he wouldn't lose his power. And he missed that power.

She was so full of love, she gave to him freely and cared for him with all her heart. She continued to sing to him as the sun rose and let a few precious rays of light into the darkness of the forest.

She brought him fresh, tender leaves to eat and brushed his fur. She picked him fresh flowers and told him stories of sunlit glades and magical things. She taught him to listen for the music from the distant meadow so they could dance in the moonlight. But what he loved best of all was *she would hold him and love him*. He had been empty for so long that she became an addiction for him. When he kissed her he would suck the very breath from her body. When she tried to pull back to catch her breath, he would get angry. He held her so tightly the magical dust wore off her wings. Soon she was afraid to fly for fear her wings wouldn't hold her.

She was afraid to be far away from him. Her light was dimming, no longer bright and strong as it used to be. For the first time in her life she felt loneliness and sadness. Love had never hurt her before. She told him her spirit was dying. She needed to be loved in a more gentle way, to get back her strength.

He knew in time she would see him for what he was. It was becoming harder and harder for him to sneak away and vent his anger and violence on the other creatures of the forest. He was afraid if she regained her light and strength she would leave him, leave him for good.

The cold blue light coming from his heart was turning darker and he caught her looking at him with suspicious eyes. Even if she hadn't accepted it yet, he knew she was seeing his darker side, which worried him even more. The more he worried the more he lied. The more she saw, the tighter he held her.

One day as he held her tightly, she lifted her hand weakly and touched the face she had come to love. "Why do you lie to me? You have no need to hide from me. I love you. You are safe with me."

He leaped to his feet, pounded his chest, gripped her tightly in his great hand. Through clenched teeth he screamed with the force of a hurricane. "Question me? You forget – this is my forest and you belong to me!"

His grip tightened, crushing her wings with no thought of the pain the little Fairy was enduring. He felt the power rushing through his veins. It excited him to see the fear in her face. She deserved to be punished. After all, he was the strongest animal in the forest and no one would tell him what to do. He must be in control. He looked at her with such hatred and contempt in his eyes and threw her to the ground. He gazed down at the pitiful creature now crumpled and broken. So what if he lost his temper? That is what his father had done to his mother and his father's father and his father before that... but a fairy is not as strong as a gorilla.

She looked at him with fear in her eyes. She didn't trust him. His light was gone. Was it ever really there? She didn't know. She couldn't understand. Why would he hurt her?

He picked her bruised and battered body up in his hand and spoke to her in his familiar tone of voice. "I am willing to forget what you have done and we can be happy just like we were in the beginning. But you will never question me!"

Her eyes lifted up to look into his face and at that moment, he knew she had changed. But in truth, she hadn't changed. She was just seeing him for the first time.

In his anger, he took her to the farthest, darkest part of the forest and put her in an abandoned sparrow's nest. He walked away, never looking back. He would leave her there and when she got lonely and scared enough she would come back to him, never to question his authority again.

Battered and bruised, her wings torn, she couldn't stop crying. Almost worse than her physical pain, her heart was broken. She couldn't understand. No one had ever treated her with so little value before.

She lay there in the dark, feeling forgotten and unloved. Did she deserve this? Was she so unlovable that she merited being be treated so badly? How could this have happened? She pulled one of the small feathers in the nest to cover her body. But the chills that raked through her would not go away. Tears coursed down her cheek.

The wind in the forest took pity on the Fairy and carried her tears and her sadness to the heavens. Just when her life force began to flicker, a single ray of light came down from above and lit up the nest. She was so weak and her pain so intense, she hardly noticed, but she sensed its warmth. She slowly opened her eyes and saw a beautiful angel looking down at her. Almost instantly there was

another and then another. They gathered around the nest and spread their wings, surrounding her in white light and love. They pulled out golden strands of their angel hair and mended her torn wings. Even the angels found it distressing to see such a delicate creature as her in this condition and they couldn't hold back their tears. As their tears fell into the nest, her body and wings were healed.

Still, the Fairy laid there, unable to move. Inside she felt so hurt and betrayed. The pain was almost too much to bear. How could she live with such pain? He'd thrown her away as if she weren't important at all. She had no value in his life and she felt she had no value in her own. The pain in her heart was so bad she thought she could not go on.

But the angels didn't give up. They wrapped their arms around her and held her in their love for days and days and weeks and weeks. They listened to her story. They whispered how they loved her and believed in her. She was valuable to them because, after all, she was the only Fairy who could see the light in everyone, no matter how small the flicker. Slowly the little Fairy found her will to live. Her life force, not as bright as it once was, held steady and became stronger every day. The angels reached down and helped the little Fairy to her feet. "It's time to leave the nest and start anew."

She was afraid. Could she ever trust again? The angels, reading her thoughts, nodded their heads and held out their hands to her and they flew to the meadow together. It felt good to have the wind on her face. It felt good to fly. She would never be exactly the same, but she felt hope.

As she flew out of the forest, there were rainbows promising tomorrow's dreams. Flowers brighter than ever were reaching out for her. Fairies, birds and friends of all kinds greeted her. At first, she was ashamed she had taken such risks to stay alone in the dark forest with a being of such little light. But she had learned so much. There were times when she missed the warmth, the strength and security of the Gorilla's arms. But then she would remember the control, isolation, and violence.

For the last time, she flew to the edge of the forest and hovered above a patch of purple irises. Tears filled her eyes for the Gorilla, whom she never saw again. She knew now that she could not make his soul well. He had to make those choices for himself. For the moment, he was not capable of that.

She felt sad that he would never know joy and love in high places, or see the light in another's eyes and feel the excitement of giving love as well as receiving it. How very sad.

The Gorilla sits at the edge of the dark forest, hidden cleverly in a bushy vine maple not far from the patch of purple irises. The grass has been worn away because of the many times he has sat here. He has told the creatures of the forest he didn't want the little Fairy anymore. She wasn't good enough for the Ruler of the Forest. He didn't have time to take care of her so he sent her away. He couldn't tell them the truth. He couldn't tell them he didn't know how to love.

It is an unusually colorful morning. Dew sparkles like diamonds, reflecting the many colors of the meadow. All seems new around her. As she flies into the morning light she says to herself and the world...

"*I AM A BELOVED DAUGHTER OF LIFE*
CAPABLE OF MY WILDEST DREAMS
LIMITED BY NO ONE!"

Facts and Resources

Battering occurs regardless of race, age, socioeconomic status, sexual orientation, mental or physical ability and religious background. Three out of every five women in this country will be beaten at some time in their lives.
A Report Describing the Initial Phase of Planning, Domestic Violence Public Education Planning Project. King County, WA, July 1993.

According to the American Medical Association, domestic violence kills as many women every five years as the total number of Americans who died in the Vietnam War.
The Domestic Violence Sourcebook, Dawn Bradley Berry. Contemporary Books, 1995.

Over 75% of the women killed from domestic violence are killed after they leave the home.
Till Violence Do Us Part, Thaemetr. Rita State Legislatures, March 1993.

In King County, Washington over 11,000 women and children were turned away from shelters because of lack of space. A large percent of women on welfare are fleeing from these situations.
Love Shouldn't Hurt, Domestic Violence Public Education Plan. State of Washington, January 13, 1994.

"He immediately puts her into a double bind. If she answers his verbal harangue, he becomes angrier with what she says. If she is quiet, her withdrawal enrages him."
The Batterer: A Psychological Profile, Donald G. Dutton, Ph.D. with Susan K. Golant. HarperCollins, 1997.

National Domestic Violence Hotline
1-800-799-SAFE